TO MY FATHER

....

Three words I'd use
to describe you : **01**

_____

_____

_____

HELLO
my name is

X _____

An activity that
makes you happy

A list of things I know
you can't live without

08

_____

_____

_____

_____

_____

_____

_____

_____

_____

_____

_____

_____

_____

09

The best story I've heard
someone tell about you

_____

_____

_____

_____

_____

_____

_____

_____

_____

_____

_____

_____

_____

_____

_____

_____

_____

10

Things you're
an expert on

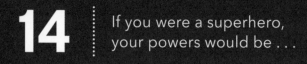

14

If you were a superhero,
your powers would be . . .

15

I'll always ask for your advice about . . .

19

When I picture
you relaxing, you are . . .

_____

_____

_____

_____

_____

_____

_____

_____

_____

_____

_____

_____

_____

_____

_____

_____

_____

_____

20

Your favorite
hobbies

A time of year
I know you enjoy

23 Your perfect weekend would include . . .

_____

_____

_____

_____

_____

_____

_____

_____

_____

_____

_____

_____

_____

_____

_____

_____

_____

_____

DAD JAMZ

A

ICE C

37 | The best birthday party
you threw for me

40

Things we used
to do together when
I was younger

_____

_____

_____

_____

_____

_____

_____

_____

_____

_____

_____

_____

_____

Our favorite things to do now

41

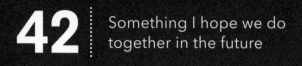

42 Something I hope we do together in the future

Things you do that show me you care | **43**

_____

_____

_____

_____

_____

_____

_____

_____

_____

_____

_____

_____

_____

44 The best gift
you ever gave me

A time when you were
especially supportive of me

48

Things you've done
to make me proud

Things I've learned from you along the way | **49**

_____

_____

_____

_____

_____

_____

_____

_____

_____

_____

_____

_____

_____

_____

50

A wish I have
for our future

Thank You
for being
My Father.